Copyright © 2019 by Jenny Weaver

Visit our website:
www.JennyWeaverWorships.com

Printed in the United States of America. All rights reserved under International Copyright Law. Contents and/or cover may not be reproduced in whole or in part.

Cover Design: Christopher Negron
Interior Design: Christopher Negron, Stacy Riddle

About the Author
Jenny Weaver
WORSHIPS

Jenny is an amazing wife, mother, author, and Holy Ghost filled worshiper of God. She believes in building families and communities in the Kingdom of God. She is best known for "Singing the Scriptures" live each week on Facebook. She reaches the nations with a heart of worship postured towards the King and, in turn, the King postures His heart towards the nations through her, bringing healing and joy to the people. Countless testimonies come in, sharing how their lives have been completely changed since watching Jenny sing the scriptures.

Once a homeless drug addict and self-cutting Wiccan, Jenny is now a true worshiper and lover of God. Transformed by His renewing power, Jenny's heart is to continue to lead people into an encounter with the Holy Spirit that will posture them in the direction of transformation and restoration.

Her inspirational testimony was picked up by TBN's Sid Roth "It's Supernatural" and "Life Today". Her first official hard copy book titled 'The Sound of Freedom' with Destiny Image Publishing Company hit shelves this year. She has a passion for teaching and leaves the people in a state of constant overflow by being obedient to the direction of God.

Jenny believes that Worship led in Spirit and in Truth, with a pure heart and no limitations, ushers in the Glory of God, which, in turn, invades the earth! It is Jenny's desire to lead Prophetic and Spontaneous High Praise Worship that releases the song of the LORD into the Hearts of the people!

"I am amazed at the hand of God on my life.
~ Jenny

FEAR IS A LIAR

This book is dedicated <u>to my students</u> in the

JW Online Academy

Your love and support have been such a blessing to me. I saw the need for this topic, because you came to me with <u>honest</u> prayer requests.

God birthed this through me just for you! Now, may many others experience the <u>freedom</u> so many of you have received from reading this!

Much Love,

Jenny

FEAR IS A LIAR

Practical Application

In this 15-Day study we are going to discuss fear and how to overcome it and live with boldness.

Everyone at one point in their lives will struggle with fear. Fear comes in many different forms and can feed into multiple areas of our lives. But God never intended for any of his children to live under the weight and burden of the spirit of fear.

For the next three weeks we are going to unpack this lesson, piece by piece, to gain a complete understanding of fear and the enemies' tactics behind it. We will dig deep into the revelation from God on how to take hold of the keys he has given us to overcome fear for good!

FEAR IS A LIAR

Table of Contents

- Day 01 – Don't Believe the Lie
- Day 02 – Becoming Aware
- Day 03 – Don't Worry 'bout a Thing!
- Day 04 – Evicted
- Day 05 – The Loudmouth Giant
- Day 06 – Godly Fear vs Satan's Fear
- Day 07 – Fear of Rejection
- Day 08 – Fear of Sickness or Death
- Day 09 – Fear of Failure
- Day 10 – Fear of Being Alone
- Day 11 – Facing Your Fears
- Day 12 – Fight from the Winning Side
- Day 13 – The Power of Perfect Love
- Day 14 – Pursue His Presence
- Day 15 – Walk it Out

FEAR IS A LIAR

Don't Believe the Lie

WHAT IS FEAR??
First and foremost, **Fear is a spirit of the enemy**!

II Timothy 1:7 (NKJV)
For God has not given us a spirit of fear, but of POWER and of LOVE and of a SOUND MIND.

Second, fear is a **LIAR**!

John 8:44 (NIV)
You belong to your father, the devil, and you want to carry out your father's desires. He was a murderer from the beginning, not holding to the truth, for there is no truth in him. When he lies, he speaks his native language, for he is a liar and the father of lies.

Fear -noun
an unpleasant emotion caused by the belief that someone or something is dangerous, likely to cause pain, or a threat. "he is prey to irrational fears"

synonyms: terror, fright, fearfulness, horror, alarm, panic, agitation, trepidation, dread, consternation, dismay, distress

I don't know about you but none of this sounds like any character traits of a Spirit filled believer to me. Yet why is it that many believers are struggling with fear in one or more areas of their lives? In fact, **almost all sin can be found rooted in fear.** The spirit of fear has been very busy working in the lives of the people, believers and non-believers alike. Causing them to not walk out their full potential in God, to get stuck, frozen in fear, to retreat, leave their post, and forsake their calling. Fear can cause doubt and double mindedness. This is one of Satan's main weapons of warfare.

One of the biggest keys to get free from fear is to acknowledge and be honest about fear in any area in your life.

FEAR IS A LIAR

Let's Get to Work

1. Make a list of your greatest fears. (write them out on paper) Note: this action does not mean you are accepting them as truth or claiming them it just means we are exposing fear in any area so the Holy Ghost can help us deal with it.

_____
_____
_____
_____

2. What are some emotions that these fear cause to rise in your life? Ex. Rage, Sadness, loneliness, terror, panic...

_____
_____
_____
_____

3. How long has this fear been active in your life?

_____
_____
_____
_____

4. Is this a generation fear that runs in your family?

_____
_____
_____
_____

FEAR IS A LIAR

Notes:

FEAR IS A LIAR

Notes:

FEAR IS A LIAR

Becoming Aware

The enemy loves to hide and stay in the dark shadows. He hates when he is exposed to the light of truth. He works overtime to plant unsound doctrine and religious restricting mindsets. All of this is rooted in fear so that he can keep people locked in demonic chains and create people who are prisoners of their own minds.

II Corinthians 2:11 (AMP)
To keep Satan from taking advantage of us; for we are not ignorant of his schemes.

Let's look at the scripture above. It tells us that, number one, Satan is trying to take advantage of us. One of the ways he does that is by causing us to be ignorant or unaware of his schemes, tactics, plans, and strategies. He does not want you to know that he is behind anxiety, fear, reluctance, doubt, rage, isolation, worry, panic, and even lack of effort. Once we become aware of the areas in our lives that the enemy has tried to bring fear we can then rightfully apply the light of truth to the situation to bring us out of that stronghold.

Psalms 55:22 (NIV)
Cast your cares on the LORD and He will sustain you; He will never let the righteous be shaken.

You cannot cast a care that is hidden or cast something you are unaware of. Jesus Confronts the lies of Fear!!

Mark 4: 39-40 (NIV)
He got up, rebuked the wind and said to the waves, "Quiet! Be still!" Then the wind died down and it was completely calm. He said to his disciples, "Why are you so afraid? Do you still have no faith?

FEAR IS A LIAR

He confronted the *root* of their fear head on and rebuked it! He then began to challenge them to confront and deal with their fear by asking them, *'why are you so afraid'*? We must ask ourselves that today!!

The storm was a lie!! It made them think that they were going to die or be harmed in some way. At the end of the day it was just a lot of noise from the enemy to cause them to doubt and not trust in the God who was with them on the boat!!

FEAR

IS A

LIAR!

FEAR IS A LIAR

Let's Get to Work

Look at the fears you wrote down yesterday and think of the outcome you believe is associated with that fear. **For Example...**

Fear of the Storm
Fear driven outcome: The boat will sink, the waves will toss me around and I will be badly hurt, we will drown.

Fear my Marriage will end
Fear driven outcome: My heart will be broken, I'll end up alone, I can't make it on my own, I'll be rejected.

1. List your Fears:
_____
_____
_____

2. What would be the possible outcome if you knew God was taking care of it?
_____
_____
_____

3. What would be the possible outcome if you knew God was taking care of it?
_____
_____
_____

4. List three areas in your life you need Faith to ARISE. In what ways would that help?
_____
_____
_____
_____

FEAR IS A LIAR

Notes:

FEAR IS A LIAR

Don't Worry 'bout a Thing

Philippians 4:6-8 (NKJV)
Be anxious for nothing, but in everything by prayer and supplication, with thanksgiving, let your requests be made known to God; and the peace of God, which surpasses all understanding, will guard your hearts and minds through Christ Jesus.

Are you ready to dive into this one today?
Worry is unfortunately a common thing that many good meaning believers are doing right now. Many times, I even hear prayer request that are wrapped with worry rather than Faith in the God of heaven and earth. The definition of worry is quite an eye opener.

worry -verb
- give way to anxiety or unease; <u>allow one's mind to dwell on difficulty or troubles</u>. "he worried about his soldier sons in the war"
- synonyms: fret, be worried, be concerned, be anxious, agonize, brood, dwell on, panic, get in a panic, lose sleep, get worked up, get in a fluster, get overwrought, be on tenterhooks;

worry -noun
- a state of anxiety and uncertainty over actual or potential problems. "they are in constant worry, for themselves as well as for their children"
- synonyms: anxiety, disturbance, perturbation, trouble, bother, distress, concern, care, upset, uneasiness, unease, disquiet, disquietude, disconcertment, fretfulness, restlessness, nervousness, nerves, agitation, edginess, tension, tenseness, stress, strain;

FEAR IS A LIAR

Take notice how it says to 'allow one's mind to **DWELL** on difficulties or trouble'. It's where you rehearse the worst-case scenarios over and over in your mind. Or you constantly think about that situation that's out of your control until it begins to disturb your spirit. **_Worry is a Joy stealer_** and **_a Peace killer_**. Where you let your mind go is up to you. The bible tells us to think on these things:

Philippians 4:8 (NASB)
Finally, brethren, whatever is true, whatever is honorable, whatever is right, whatever is pure, whatever is lovely, whatever is of good repute, if there is any excellence and if anything, worthy of praise, dwell on these things.

Steer your thoughts **AWAY** from fear based and worrisome thoughts, remember it's in your hands. This takes practice but you can do all things through Christ who strengthens you.

FEAR IS A LIAR

Let's Get to Work

1. If fear comes to your mind today in any way, shape or form, ask yourself these questions:

    - Is this **True**?
    - Is this **Honorable**?
    - Is this **Right**?
    - Is this **Pure**?
    - Is this **Lovely**?
    - Is this a **Good Report**?
    - Is this **Excellent**?
    - Is this **Worthy of Praise**

2. How do your thoughts about that specific situation match up?

    _____
    _____
    _____
    _____
    _____

3. List three replacement thoughts for fear-based thoughts.

    _____
    _____
    _____
    _____

FEAR IS A LIAR

Notes:

FEAR IS A LIAR

Evicted

Ok, so for the last three days we have talked about the different ways that fear tries to come in and where it comes from. Today I want to steer you and motivate you to **draw a line in the sand** and **say no more fear in my life!** It is time that the people of God stand up and **evict fear** from our homes, our children, our cities, and in our own lives.

In my life I struggled for years with the spirit of fear. I was so afraid at nighttime especially. I was afraid to step out into new things; I was afraid of being rejected and letting people down. Fear had taken over my life in such a way that **I identified my own personality and characteristics from a place of fear.**

Once the LORD began to take me through my process of restoration, he began to deal with that spirit in my life. He brought me into the revelation of his word and the Holy Spirit helped me to apply the word to my life to overcome fear. He didn't just come in and remove it, but He **exposed it** in my life and empowered me to **resist** the spirit of fear and **make him flee**. I remember getting so tired of being scared I stood up one night and I said "**In the name of Jesus Christ, You! spirit of fear get out of here right now!**" I began to **understand that I had the authority over the devil** in my life. I began to understand the power of the blood of Jesus. I began to understand God's perfect love for me and that is what casts out all fear.

Psalm 27:1 (NIV)
The LORD is my light and my salvation -- whom shall I fear? The LORD is the stronghold of my life -- of whom shall I be afraid?

FEAR IS A LIAR

Look at the scripture above and ask yourself those same questions today. If the LORD is truly your light and is truly your salvation, what on earth is there to fear? Stand up today and begin to evict fear out of your emotions, out of your heart, out of your mind, and out of your spirit in the name of Jesus!

Matthew 20:1 (NIV)
Jesus called his twelve disciples together and gave them authority to cast out evil spirits and to heal every kind of disease and illness.

He did NOT tell them to counsel, get along with or learn to deal with evil spirits – He gave them authority to CAST THEM OUT!!! Praise the LORD, I get excited about that.

FEAR IS A LIAR

Let's Get to Work

1. What three things does Psalms 27:1 say that God is?
_____
_____
_____
_____
_____

2. What does it mean by 'the stronghold of my life'?
_____
_____
_____
_____
_____

3. How does 'the Light of God and His salvation' give us reason not to fear?
_____
_____
_____
_____
_____

FEAR IS A LIAR

Notes:

FEAR IS A LIAR

The Loudmouth Giant

The title of the study is called 'Fear is a Liar' for a reason. I want you to understand that fear is based on lies from the enemy. Someone once said that fear stands for: **False Evidence Appearing Real**. Fear is like a big loud-mouth giant bully trying to keep the sons and daughters of God under its' thumb. Let's look at the story of David and Goliath today.

1 Samuel 17:8-11 (NIV)
Goliath stood and shouted to the ranks of Israel, "Why do you come out and line up for battle? Am I not a Philistine, and are you not the servants of Saul? Choose a man and have him come down to me." If he is able to fight and kill me, we will become your subjects; but if I overcome him and kill him, you will become our subjects and serve us." Then the Philistine said, "This day I defy the armies of Israel! Give me a man and let us fight each other." On hearing the Philistine's words, Saul and all the Israelites were dismayed and terrified.

Notice what happened in **verse 11**! It says, upon hearing the giants' threats Saul and every one of **the Israelites were terrified**!!! Just because of words! They weren't fighting yet or being physically pushed back by war combat; they were dismayed and terrified upon hearing threats and intimidation from the enemy. This is the enemy's tactic he is constantly yelling intimidating and threatening things to the minds into the hearts of people all over the world. He tells them they aren't good enough, they aren't qualified enough, they don't have enough resources, that they will look silly if they step out. That he is going to take things from them, and they won't ever get well; God isn't listening to them and the list of lies goes on and on. What's interesting to me is that Saul and all the Israelites **gave their ear over to the enemy**. They knew he had their full attention and begin to use mental warfare against them. But if they were seeking God for the strategy and tuning out the loud-mouth giant then those fiery darts would not have been able to penetrate their hearts.

FEAR IS A LIAR

Think about it...

Be careful who you listen to! The Bible says, '*my sheep know my voice and a strangers voice they will run from.*' **Goliath represents a spirit of fear in our lives.** He taunted and tormented them with His words. He kept trying to make himself sound undefeatable. He had empty threats. Notice he said, 'you will become our subjects and serve us.' **Fear wants to be a master over you.** It wants you to become its slave and do what it wants you to do and behave the way it wants you to behave. But **you can't serve two masters** the bible says. You must choose to **silence this loud-mouth giant** once and for all!

F: False

E: Evidence

A: Appearing

R: Real

FEAR IS A LIAR

Let's Get to Work

1. What are some of the intimidating things the enemy has been telling you?

_____
_____
_____
_____

2. Have you given your ear over to the enemy? If so, what are some things you can do to re-focus your attention back on the Father's voice only?

_____
_____
_____
_____

FEAR IS A LIAR

Notes:

FEAR IS A LIAR

Godly Fear vs Satan's Fear

Not all fear is bad!
The Bible instructs us to fear the LORD. That word fear does not mean to be scared to go to Him or be scared of Him but to have a reference so strong for His Holiness and his infinite power. It's like the highest level of respect for His Kingship.

Proverbs 1:7 (NIV)
The fear of the LORD is the beginning of knowledge, but fools despise wisdom and instruction.

Hosea 4:6 (NIV)
My people are destroyed for lack of knowledge. Because you have rejected knowledge, I also will reject you from being priest for me; Because you have forgotten the law of your God, I also will forget your children.

Proverbs 9:10 (NIV)
The fear of the LORD is the beginning of wisdom, And the knowledge of the Holy One is understanding.

Someone who fears the LORD is wise. Someone who does not have a holy fear of God is foolish. More and more we are seeing the fear of God diminish around the world. There was a time when you wouldn't see the things on the news that you see nowadays. There was a time that even sinners were reverent when it came to the church and the things of God. But God wants to restore the fear of the LORD back to his people. A healthy fear. A Godly fear.

The fear of the LORD will cause a person to live upright, holy and righteous before the King of Kings and the LORD of Lords. The fear of the LORD will cause someone to cast down our idols and have reverence and respect for the risen Messiah. The fear of the LORD will cause someone to obey his commandments in love. Some people have miss used the word of God and have taught with ungodly fear tactics to try to win people to Christ. The Bible tells us to test the spirits. The Bible tells us to train up our senses to know and to discern good from evil. Godly fear will lead you to a deeper relationship in Christ Jesus. Satan's fear will lead you straight into bondage.

FEAR IS A LIAR

Let's Get to Work

1. What is the beginning of wisdom?

2. What destroys people spiritually and/or physically according to Hosea 4:6?

3. What is an example of having a fear of the LORD?

FEAR IS A LIAR

Notes:

FEAR IS A LIAR

Notes:

FEAR IS A LIAR

Fear of Rejection

This one is a big one for many believers. Rejection is going to happen to us all at one point, but we don't have to live in fear of it. It doesn't have to become our identity.

We all have a natural desire to want to be accepted and loved by others. The enemy will try to come in with the fear of being rejected and use this as a tool to fuel toxic, unhealthy, ungodly mindsets and behaviors in people. When I travel and minister, I find that fear is one of the main issues that people and are in need of deliverance from.

A spirit of fear working through rejection causes believers to be more concerned about the opinions of men rather than the opinion of our Heavenly Father. It causes people to get stuck, terrified of moving forward in their God given assignments.

It causes them to post certain things, say certain things or to do certain things to gain a level of attention that will satisfy their craving to be accepted.

We live in the age of social media and we see how the fear of rejection is operating in a major way. Many people will post a picture or a status and will wait to see if it is liked by other people, and if it is not liked like they expect they perceive that as being rejected. They will then delete it and internalize it. I've seen fear manifest in people when they're not given a level of attention or engagement they desire and they will unfriend, unfollow or think that they have done something wrong. It becomes a tormenting mindset that is rooted in rejection. It causes people to view things in such a flawed way. Things like body image, gifting, and personality.

FEAR IS A LIAR

Some might even find their choices are flawed because they don't think they will be accepted or loved by other people unless they follow the crowd. Many people that are suffering with the fear of rejection live in a prison of torment. The only way to get free is to **seek God in such a passionate way every single day** so that the revelation of God's love begins to form your identity solely in Christ. Study out the word of Truth so that it can dismantle every lie from the pits of hell. Begin to decree the Word of the LORD over your life and reject any deceiving thought that would try to come. Command that demonic spirit to go from your heart, your mind and your soul, in Jesus name.

FEAR IS A LIAR

Let's Get to Work

1. Do you struggle with fear of rejection? If yes, complete question two

_____
_____
_____
_____

2. At what age did this start?

_____
_____
_____
_____

3. What are three things God says about you according to the bible?

_____
_____
_____
_____

1. What are three things you can use against the lies of the enemy when he brings up feeling of being rejected?

_____
_____
_____
_____

FEAR IS A LIAR

Notes:

FEAR IS A LIAR

Fear of Sickness or Death

We have established that fear is a spirit and fear is a liar. Yet so many people are still in bondage to fear regarding their health and their future. One of the greatest stories in the Bible talks about the threat of death and harm from the enemy and what it did to one of the greatest men of God in that day.

1 Kings 19
Now Ahab told Jezebel everything Elijah had done and how he had killed all the prophets with the sword. So, Jezebel sent a messenger to Elijah to say, "May the gods deal with me, be it ever so severely, if by this time tomorrow I do not make your life like that of one of them."

1 Kings 19:1-9 (NIV)

Elijah was afraid and ran for his life! When he came to Beersheba in Judah, he left his servant there, while he himself went a day's journey into the wilderness. He came to a broom bush, sat down under it and prayed that he might die. "I have had enough, LORD," he said. "Take my life; I am no better than my ancestors." Then he lay down under the bush and fell asleep. All at once an angel touched him and said, "Get up and eat." He looked around, and there by his head was some bread baked over hot coals, and a jar of water. He ate and drank and then lay down again. The angel of the LORD came back a second time and touched him and said, "Get up and eat, for the journey is too much for you." So, he got up and ate and drank. Strengthened by that food, he traveled forty days and forty nights until he reached Horeb, the mountain of God. There he went into a cave and spent the night. And the word of the LORD came to him: "What are you doing here, Elijah?"

FEAR IS A LIAR

This story is absolutely incredible because it follows one of the greatest victories in the whole Bible. When Elijah prayed and called down fire from heaven, burnt up the altar and all the people saw it, they turned back to God!! He should've been even more empowered by that amazing miracle that he just witnessed and was a part of. But before he could even shout the victory the enemy came in with threats of death and harm and the Bible says that Elijah was afraid. Then it says he ran for his life and hid and even began to desire death for his own life.

Have you ever been in the hospital room and you're waiting on results and all of a sudden and you begin to get nervous about what they are going to come back and say? Have you ever received a report from the doctor that said you have a disease or sickness, something that is not supposed to be in the body of a believer and it began to bring fear in your life? Have you ever feared death so much that you're afraid of things like flying or stepping out of your comfort zone? Fear of death and sickness comes to rob God's people of their right to healing and their right to have life and to have it more abundantly.

Let's look at our scriptures for today and see how he was able to overcome this fear.

It says the angel of the LORD came to him and gave him bread and water that symbolizes the word of God which we know is the bread of life and water symbolizes the Holy Spirit. You have to combat those thoughts of fear with a true foundation in the word of God and be filled with his spirit. You literally have to study the word of God and think of it as the bread that is feeding your spirit and your soul. You wouldn't go days and days without food and not realize it, so you shouldn't go days and day without studying and reading the word of God and not realize it.

FEAR IS A LIAR

Let's Get to Work

1. What drove Elijah into the wilderness?

_____
_____
_____
_____

2. Do you think fear of being sick comes from a lack of trust or faith? Explain…

_____
_____
_____
_____

3. Does sickness come from God? Explain and/or find a scripture reference supporting your answer?

_____
_____
_____
_____

FEAR IS A LIAR

Notes:

FEAR IS A LIAR

Fear of Failure

The prodigal son story is such a great example of this particular fear and the beautiful ending of how perfect love conquered it.

Luke 15:11-24 (NIV)
The Parable of the Lost Son
Jesus continued: "There was a man who had two sons. The younger one said to his father, 'father, give me my share of the estate.' So, he divided his property between them. "Not long after that, the younger son got together all he had, set off for a distant country and there squandered his wealth in wild living. After he had spent everything, there was a severe famine in that whole country, and he began to be in need. So he went and hired himself out to a citizen of that country, who sent him to his fields to feed pigs. He longed to fill his stomach with the pods that the pigs were eating, but no one gave him anything. "When he came to his senses, he said, 'How many of my father's hired servants have food to spare, and here I am starving to death! I will set out and go back to my father and say to him: Father, I have sinned against heaven and against you. I am no longer worthy to be called your son; make me like one of your hired servants.' So he got up and went to his father. "But while he was still a long way off, his father saw him and was filled with compassion for him; he ran to his son, threw his arms around him and kissed him. "The son said to him, 'father, I have sinned against heaven and against you. I am no longer worthy to be called your son.' "But the father said to his servants, 'Quick! Bring the best robe and put it on him. Put a ring on his finger and sandals on his feet. Bring the fattened calf and kill it. Let's have a feast and celebrate. For this son of mine was dead and is alive again; he was lost and is found.' So, they began to celebrate.

Luke 15:12 (NIV)
The younger one said to his father, 'Father, give me my share of the estate.' So, he divided his property between them. "Not long after that, the younger son got together all he had, set off for a distant country...

FEAR IS A LIAR

*Pause and reflect - notice how he wanted what was his and set out to most likely show that he would be successful. 'I'm certain he didn't plan to fail or lose all he had. --...and there squandered his wealth in wild living. 14 After he had spent everything, there was a severe famine in that whole country, and he began to be in need.

*Pause and reflect - notice how his plans went south, and all of a sudden he was in the midst of a terrible situation that he didn't know how to get out of. Look at his actions that are driven next by this fear. -- 15 So he went and hired himself out to a citizen of that country, who sent him to his fields to feed pigs.

*Pause and reflect - why in the world didn't he just go home at that point? Here you can clearly see fear of failure operating. What was he trying to do by accepting such a job? ---- gain back some of what he lost so he would look like a failure. --17 "When he came to his senses, he said, 'How many of my father's hired servants have food to spare, and here I am starving to death! 18 I will set out and go back to my father...

*Pause and reflect - Here we see the beginning of his deliverance out of the situation beginning to happen and it starts with recognizing the condition he was in and setting out to get back to his father. -- and say to him: father, I have sinned against heaven and against you. 19 I am no longer worthy to be called your son; make me like one of your hired servants.'

*Pause and reflect- his idea to go to the father was right but even in that right motive was fear of rejection and failure still operating and we see that by his statement that he isn't worthy to be a son and comes up with a better title for himself as a servant. 20 So he got up and went to his father.

REFLECT- Although he had some 'stinking thinking' about who he was and his future, he still used wisdom and GOT UP- got up out of his pain -- got up out of his misery -- got up out of his present situation and took a step forward towards his father. He went to his father even in the condition and state of mind that he was in. He knew that being close to the father would fix his current situation. And he understood that being away from his father caused things to get worse.

FEAR IS A LIAR

Let's Get to Work

1. Time for a heart check -- where are you when it comes to the Father? (a far off, headed towards Him, in the house already?)

_____
_____
_____
_____

2. Have you discovered a possible fear of failure happening in your life?

_____
_____
_____
_____

3. How can staying next to the Father give you the confidence to know who you are even if you fail at something?

_____
_____
_____
_____

FEAR IS A LIAR

Notes:

FEAR IS A LIAR

A Fear of Being Alone

- "No one understands me"
- "I have no one that has my back."
- "I'm going through this all by myself"
- "I'm all alone in this situation"

Have you ever had any of these thoughts above? These are the lies that the enemy will feed someone to instill in their heart a fear of being alone. We all long to be in fellowship with other people. God placed a desire for us to have fellowship and family because that is his nature as well. The enemy will use a natural longing for fellowship and twist it so that it becomes a fear of being alone. He uses this as a tactic to keep God's people in bondage.

In our age of social media and the huge focus on connecting to other people can and some ways be a good thing, but if you're struggling with a fear of being lonely it can sometimes take a toll on a person. Seeing everyone else married and living a great Life can make someone struggling with this feel even more alone. Sometimes it can make someone feel left out, enforcing these feelings of loneliness even more. The way to combat the fear of being alone and to shut the mouth of the liar to gain an unshakable confidence in your identity as a part of the kingdom of God, a part of a very large loving and supporting family. It's interesting to me that the fear of being alone can cause someone to have such erratic behavior and almost aggressive like responses to other people and a very clingy way that it actually causes the very thing that they set out not to have happen, happen. I recognize immediately that this is a tactic of the enemy this fear is, often times, coupled with the fear of being rejected. The truth of the matter is that we are never alone because the Holy Spirit Jesus Christ and Father God are always with us and they have determined before the foundations of the earth for us to connect to certain people at certain times in our lives for certain seasons and if we are abiding in Christ then he will lead us to having right fellowship right alignments and right connections all throughout our lives.

FEAR IS A LIAR

Let's Get to Work

1. Have you ever dealt with feelings of loneliness?

_____
_____
_____
_____

2. Do you still struggle in this area? If yes, write about it. If no, what's something that helped you get free from this?

_____
_____
_____
_____

3. Facts!! Find three scriptures that give you hope that you are not alone.

_____
_____
_____
_____

FEAR IS A LIAR

Facing Your Fears

There must come a time when you face fear head on -- no more hiding! Let's look again at the story of David and Goliath because I believe it paints a glorious picture of how to win the battle against fear.

1 Samuel 17:32-40 (NIV)
David said to Saul, "Let no one lose heart on account of this Philistine; your servant will go and fight him." Saul replied, "You are not able to go out against this Philistine and fight him; you are only a young man, and he has been a warrior from his youth." But David said to Saul, "Your servant has been keeping his father's sheep. When a lion or a bear came and carried off a sheep from the flock, I went after it, struck it and rescued the sheep from its mouth. When it turned on me, I seized it by its hair, struck it and killed it. Your servant has killed both the lion and the bear; this uncircumcised Philistine will be like one of them, because he has defied the armies of the living God. The LORD who rescued me from the paw of the lion and the paw of the bear will rescue me from the hand of this Philistine." Saul said to David, "Go, and the LORD be with you." Then Saul dressed David in his own tunic. He put a coat of armor on him and a bronze helmet on his head. David fastened on his sword over the tunic and tried walking around, because he was not used to them. "I cannot go in these," he said to Saul, "because I am not used to them." So, he took them off. Then he took his staff in his hand, chose five smooth stones from the stream, put them in the pouch of his shepherd's bag and, with his sling in his hand, approached the Philistine.

The Bible tells us that for 40 days the Israelites listened to Goliath as he threw insults against God, bullied them and hurled fear and torment their way. The fear was so great that no one in that army was willing to stand up and fight Goliath head on.

FEAR IS A LIAR

The story tells us that here comes David a very young boy whose job was to look over the sheep. He comes to the battlefield and sees the Israelites lining up in their places to fight against the Philistines and once again Goliath comes out and throws insults and intimidation coupled with death threats and the Israelites flea in fear.

When David hears the tactics of the enemy, there was a boldness and zeal for the LORD that rises up in him and he stands up, says that he will fight this Philistine on behalf of the LORD. He is immediately told that he doesn't have what it takes to fight this evil, yet he does not get discouraged by King Saul's estimate of his strength because he knows his strength lies in the hands of the LORD.

He then boldly begins to recall all the times that he was able to win the battle over the enemy and reminds himself and King Saul that God has always been with him and if he was able to defeat the lion and the bear then he was certainly able to defeat a loud mouth giant who spoke against the Almighty God. Verse 40 says that with his sling shot in his hand, he approached the Philistine. He faced the giant with confidence that he would have the victory because God was going to fight this battle for him.

No matter what you're facing today no matter what strategy the enemy has tried to come against you with in the area of fear today is the day that we face of fear in the name of Jesus! Today's the day that we pull out the rock of our salvation we use it to defeat Satan and all of his lies.

FEAR IS A LIAR

Let's Get to Work

1. Why did Saul assume David couldn't fight Goliath? What things was he looking at?

_____
_____
_____
_____

2. Where did David gain such a confidence to fight lions, bears and a giant?

_____
_____
_____
_____

3. Why is it good to reflect back on all the things you've been able to overcome?

_____
_____
_____
_____

4. List as many things as you can that God has brought you through, that you have defeated through Him and things you've been freed from.

_____
_____
_____
_____

FEAR IS A LIAR

Notes:

FEAR IS A LIAR

Fight from the Winning Side

Today, I'm going to give you a key that's going to help you successfully maintain the victory over at any fear in your life. And that key is to always no matter what fight from the winning side! Let's get back to our story of David and Goliath and find out exactly what this key means.

I Samuel 17:41-52 (NIV)
Meanwhile, the Philistine, with his shield bearer in front of him, kept coming closer to David. He looked David over and saw that he was little more than a boy, glowing with health and handsome, and he despised him. He said to David, "Am I a dog, that you come at me with sticks?" And the Philistine cursed David by his gods. "Come here," he said, "and I'll give your flesh to the birds and the wild animals!" David said to the Philistine, "You come against me with sword and spear and javelin, but I come against you in the name of the LORD Almighty, the God of the armies of Israel, whom you have defied. This day the LORD will deliver you into my hands, and I'll strike you down and cut off your head. This very day I will give the carcasses of the Philistine army to the birds and the wild animals, and the whole world will know that there is a God in Israel. All those gathered here will know that it is not by sword or spear that the LORD saves; for the battle is the LORD's, and he will give all of you into our hands." As the Philistine moved closer to attack him, David ran quickly toward the battle line to meet him. Reaching into his bag and taking out a stone, he slung it and struck the Philistine on the forehead. The stone sank into his forehead, and he fell face down on the ground. So, David triumphed over the Philistine with a sling and a stone; without a sword in his hand he struck down the Philistine and killed him. David ran and stood over him. He took hold of the Philistine's sword and drew it from the sheath. After he killed him, he cut off his head with the sword. When the Philistines saw that their hero was dead, they turned and ran. Then the men of Israel and Judah surged forward with a shout and pursued the Philistines to the entrance of Gath and to the gates of Ekron.

FEAR IS A LIAR

Here we see that Goliath moved a little bit closer to David but then he calls to David once he can finally get a good look at him and tells David to come closer to where he is. It also says that he had his shield bearer in front of him. Why in the world would he not just overtake David? Why in the world is this great conqueror being let around by shield bearer? Why is he calling for David to come to him? If I may insert some thought-provoking ideas. Goliath, we know was a giant. Giants are not fictional characters it is a real syndrome that still occurs to some people even today. To understand how to win the battle I feel it's important to know your enemies' weaknesses. As well as your own strengths to fight and to win. Giants have a syndrome called Gigantism. It's basically when tumor grows on the pituitary gland, the gland makes far more growth hormone than the body needs.

Some of the symptoms of Gigantism that occur are:

- **Very large hands and feet**
- **Thick toes and fingers**
- **A prominent jaw and forehead**
- **Coarse facial features**
- **Excessive sweating**
- **Severe or recurrent headaches**
- **Weakness**
- **Insomnia and other sleep disorders**
- **Deafness**
- **Loss of sight or tunnel vision**

I wonder if the Israelites truly knew that their enemy was so weak and so fatigued from insomnia that he had to have someone else hold up his shield for him? I wonder if the Israelites knew that Goliath suffered with eyesight issues and was barely able to see or hearing issues and had to have this shield bearer lead him around? Lastly, I wonder if they knew all of these things would they have still fled in fear? The enemy is NOT equipped to win the battle, all he has is his big mouth and his threats. He is weak, He doesn't have a spiritual advantage, he can't see the way we see, he can't hear with Kingdom ears, he is a tormented soul that has no rest, he has the appearance of being big and bad but the reality is he is a defeated loser!!

FEAR IS A LIAR

Let's Get to Work

1. Looks can be deceiving. List some ways the enemy convinces people he is to be feared.

_____
_____
_____
_____
_____

2. Why was David the only one there who stood up to Goliath? Do you think he saw Goliath different than the others?

_____
_____
_____
_____
_____

3. David was upset that this Giant was hurling insults against the God of Israel and was determined to shut the Giants mouth once and for all. What was the prophetic decree he declared over Goliath that day?

_____
_____
_____

FEAR IS A LIAR

Notes:

FEAR IS A LIAR

The Power of Perfect Love

The way to drive out ALL fear is **to be made perfect in Love.** Let's explore what that means today.

"If anyone acknowledges that Jesus is the Son of God, God lives in them and they in God. And so, we know and rely on the love God has for us. God is love. Whoever lives in love lives in God, and God in them. This is how love is made complete among us so that we will have confidence on the day of judgment: In this world we are like Jesus. **There is no fear in love. But perfect love drives out fear, because fear has to do with punishment. The one who fears is not made perfect in love.**

1 John 4:15-19 (NIV)
We love because he first loved us.

Does God love? **He IS LOVE!** Wow! What a statement that not only does he love but he actually is love and what we consider love is a part of his very nature and came directly from him.

These a few scriptures are so beautiful as they illustrate to us that we are to rely on God's love for us. In your daily life do you rely on God's infinite and amazing love to get you through everything that you might be going through? We must learn to receive the Father's love for us every day. We must learn how to receive love from other brothers and sisters in Christ. We must learn how to receive love in the way the Bible intends for us from our spouses and family members. And it all starts first in for most with knowing that God loves us with an unconditional love I love that is truly hard to even put into our own English language.

FEAR IS A LIAR

The scripture is very much to the point and says there is no fear not an ounce not a drop not a trace in love and then gives an eye-opening statement and says someone that fears have not been made perfect in God's love. Meaning has not received completely the revelation of the love of God for them in their lives. Because once his perfect love is in embraced and received completely it cast out all fear from the minds of God's children and from the hearts of His children. Peter has a beautiful story of how perfect love canceled out fear in his life. We all know that he denied Christ for fear of harm and or death so let's look at that scripture reference today.

Luke 22:54-62 (NIV)
Peter was following at a distance. And when they had kindled a fire in the middle of the courtyard and sat down together, Peter sat down among them. Then a servant girl, seeing him as he sat in the light and looking closely at him, said, "This man also was with him." But he denied it, saying, "Woman, I do not know him." And a little later someone else saw him and said, "You also are one of them." But Peter said, "Man, I am not." And after an interval of about an hour still another insisted, saying, "Certainly this man also was with him, for he too is a Galilean." But Peter said, "Man, I do not know what you are talking about." And immediately, while he was still speaking, the rooster crowed. And the LORD turned and looked at Peter. And Peter remembered the saying of the LORD, how he had said to him, "Before the rooster crows today, you will deny me three times." And he went out and wept bitterly."

FEAR IS A LIAR

Peter previously told the LORD that he would never leave him but upon being faced with everything that had happened that night fear begin to grip his life. Fear of the unknown what would happen to him, fear of being harmed and taken into prison and fear of possible death caused him to deny who he was step away from his own identity as a follower of Christ follow Jesus not closely but at a distance and then be overwhelmed with shame and guilt. When Jesus rose again and begin to appear to the disciples the beautiful thing that Peter did was run to Jesus. Just like we saw the prodigal come to his senses get up and go directly to his father Peter also in spite of his failures in spite of his mistakes in spite of the condemnation and guilt he ran to Jesus. This is what we must do to truly see the manifestation of perfect love in our lives. I love how Jesus has a conversation with Peter and allows that perfect love and Peter's confession of love to cancel out his previous confessions of denying Christ. Let's look at when they finished eating...

John 21:15-17 (NIV)
Jesus said to Simon Peter, "Simon son of John, do you love me more than these? "Yes, LORD," he said, "you know that I love you." Jesus said, "Feed my lambs." Again, Jesus said, "Simon son of John, do you love me?" He answered, "Yes, LORD, you know that I love you." Jesus said, "Take care of my sheep." The third time he said to him, "Simon son of John, do you love me?" Peter was hurt because Jesus asked him the third time, "Do you love me?" He said, "LORD, you know all things; you know that I love you." Jesus said, "Feed my sheep."

Three times Peter was afraid, fear breathing down his neck and he denied Jesus and he denied who he was and his calling. But Jesus and his perfect love wanted so much to restore Peter and he gave them a chance to realize his love for the LORD and Jesus gave him his assignment back with every confession and said feed my sheep. Peter would go on to doing that very thing with no fear he stood up on the day of Pentecost and declare Jesus to so many people and saw thousands give their lives to Christ right there. There is no fear in the perfect love of Jesus.

FEAR IS A LIAR

Let's Get to Work

1. When Peter denied Jesus what fear do you think was operating at that point? Explain.

_____
_____
_____
_____

2. Luke 22:62 Says Once he realized what he did he went outside and wept bitterly (a very deep cry). What do you think what's happening there? Fear? Shame? Conviction? Failure?

_____
_____
_____
_____

3. Why did Jesus have Peter confess out loud his love for Him 3 times?

_____
_____
_____
_____

4. How does knowing Gods love make you free from fear?

_____
_____
_____
_____

FEAR IS A LIAR

Pursue His Presence

Have you ever been in a church service and been completely overwhelmed by the presence of God? Or have you ever been in your secret place or even in your car and had the presence of God come in in such a mighty way that you'll remember it forever? And in that moment where are you afraid of the bills not being paid? Most likely you weren't even thinking of that. Were you afraid of your marriage falling apart? I doubt that was even in your mind. I don't mean just a few goosebumps because a very good song is on I'm talking about the tangible presence of God. It takes us outside of our natural circumstances and places us into the supernatural realm where we are now seated in heavenly places and we are looking at the situation with an eagle I view. The Bible says that in his presence is fullness of joy. I've never seen someone that is full of joy and terrified all at the same. Jesus teaches about worry and fear and what we are to do instead of it.

Matthew 6:25-34 (NIV)
25 "Therefore I tell you, do not worry about your life, what you will eat or drink; or about your body, what you will wear. Is not life more than food, and the body more than clothes? 26 Look at the birds of the air; they do not sow or reap or store away in barns, and yet your heavenly Father feeds them. Are you not much more valuable than they? 27 Can any one of you by worrying add a single hour to your life? 28 "And why do you worry about clothes? See how the flowers of the field grow. They do not labor or spin. 29 Yet I tell you that not even Solomon in all his splendor was dressed like one of these. 30 If that is how God clothes the grass of the field, which is here today and tomorrow is thrown into the fire, will he not much more clothe you—you of little faith? 31 So do not worry, saying, 'What shall we eat?' or 'What shall we drink?' or 'What shall we wear?' 32 For the pagans run after all these things, and your heavenly Father knows that you need them. 33 But seek first his kingdom and his righteousness, and all these things will be given to you as well. 34 Therefore do not worry about tomorrow, for tomorrow will worry about itself. Each day has enough trouble of its own.

FEAR IS A LIAR

Jesus not only addresses the foolishness of worrying but enforces your value and the Father's love toward you which we all know is the perfect love that cast out the fear. When I know my Father takes care of me and loves me so much, I do not fear my bills not being paid. I don't fear dying of a disease. I don't fear being alone because I know that he'll never leave or for sake me. I don't fear the threats and attacks of the enemy because I know that I don't fight flesh and blood but it's the devil that's trying to come against me so I put on the full armor I stand in his love and I see the salvation of the LORD.

Seek First Seek First Seek First

Once we get that everything else falls into place. It's the most beautiful arrangement and covenant that we have. My job is to just sit at the feet of Jesus and be a daughter. Your job is to see God sit at his feet trust him and be his child and all the cares of this life fade away.

FEAR IS A LIAR

The lyrics of this song say it best...

Turn your eyes upon Jesus

O soul are you weary and troubled?
No light in the darkness you see?
There's light for a look at the Savior
And life more abundant and free
Turn your eyes upon Jesus
Look full in His wonderful face
And the things of earth will grow strangely dim
In the light of His glory and grace
Through death into life everlasting
He passed, and we follow Him there
Over us sin no more hath dominion
For more than conquerors we are
And turn your eyes upon Jesus
Look full in His wonderful face
And the things of earth will grow strangely dim
In the light of His glory and grace
His word shall not fail you, He promised
Believe Him and all will be well
Then go to a world that is dying
His perfect salvation to tell
And turn your eyes upon Jesus
Look full in His wonderful face
And the things of earth will grow strangely dim
In the light of His Glory and Grace

FEAR IS A LIAR

Notes:

FEAR IS A LIAR

Let's Get to Work

1. What are the five things Jesus says not to worry over?

_____
_____
_____
_____

2. What two things in nature did He use to show an example of trusting Him?

_____
_____
_____
_____

3. What did Jesus say was the root of worry? Vs. 30

_____
_____
_____
_____

4. What are some things you can do to build up your faith?

_____
_____
_____
_____

FEAR IS A LIAR

Notes:

FEAR IS A LIAR

Walk it Out

Now that you are at the very last day, I want to just encourage you to continue with got to start it in your heart and in your life. I trust that through this study God has revealed areas of fear that he is wanting to deal with, and he has given you the tools and the keys to have victory every day.

Now, go forth and boldness like Little David when you face the giant. Go forth in your assignment like Peter when he went on to preach the gospel and to turn the world upside down. Go forth in your identity as a true Child of the most high just like the prodigal who got up and ran to his father and receive the robe the ring the shoes and the feast prepared only for co-heir and go forth in your own unique identity chosen called anointed appointed for such a time as this!! This is a walk of faith. This is a walk of trust. This is a walk of love. It's time we walk with boldness, victory and authority!

FEAR IS A LIAR

Let's Get to Work

1. The bible says where the Spirit of the LORD is there is _____.

2. In His presence is _____.

3. Whom the son sets free _____.

4. You shall know the truth and _____.

5. Fear not for I have redeemed you _____.

6. No weapon formed _____.

7. Perfect love _____.

8. I am more than _____.

9. By His stripes _____.

FEAR IS A LIAR

Notes:

FEAR IS A LIAR

Notes:

FEAR IS A LIAR

Notes:

FEAR IS A LIAR

Notes:

FEAR IS A LIAR

Notes:

FEAR IS A LIAR

Notes:

FEAR IS A LIAR

Notes:

FEAR IS A LIAR

Notes:

FEAR IS A LIAR

Notes:

FEAR IS A LIAR

Notes:

FEAR IS A LIAR

Notes:

Books By Jenny

For more info. visit
JennyWeaverWorships.com

Made in the USA
Columbia, SC
07 January 2021